CLOTHES

IN HOT AND COLD PLACES

SIMON CRISP

Wayland

TITLES IN THIS SERIES

Animals in Hot and Cold Places
Clothes in Hot and Cold Places
Food and Farming in Hot and Cold Places
Homes in Hot and Cold Places

Series editor: Geraldine Purcell
Series designer: Helen White

Cover: (top) These Inuit children are wrapped up against the cold in their warm, fur outfits. (bottom) These Indian women are wearing brightly coloured saris which will protect them from the hot sun and help to keep them cool.
Title page: Skiers' clothes protect them from the cold.

First published in 1994 by Wayland (Publishers) Limited
61 Western Road, Hove, East Sussex BN3 1JD

British Library Cataloguing in Publication Data
Crisp, Simon
  Clothes in Hot and Cold Places. – (Hot & Cold Series)
  I. Title II. Price, David III. Series 391

ISBN 0 7502 0717 5

Typeset by White Design
Printed and bound in Great Britain by BPCC Paulton Books Ltd., Paulton

CONTENTS

WHY WEAR CLOTHES?

▲ These Inuit children on Baffin Island, Canada, are wearing warm, fur outfits with hoods and gloves to protect them from the cold, snowy weather.

We wear clothes for many different reasons. The main reason is to keep us warm when it is cold and cool when it is hot. It is important that our body temperature is kept at a steady level. If we get too cold our bodies stop working properly and we die. Our bodies also need protection from the heat of the sun. In very hot places, if people get too hot their bodies can become dehydrated (lose too much water). If this happens they could die.

Clothing can help us control how hot or cold we feel. If we are cold we put more clothes on, but if we are too hot we take some clothes off until we feel comfortable again.

You may think that if wearing less clothing keeps the body cool, people living in hot countries must wear few clothes. This is not always the case. In some hot countries people wear clothes that cover their bodies because it is considered decent, or correct, to do so. Some people wear certain clothes because of their religion. For instance, Muslim women in the Middle East and North Africa cover themselves almost completely.

People do not just wear clothes for protection against the heat and cold. All over the world people like to wear clothes that make them look good. Think about the clothes you wear. Do you like certain colours or styles?

In some countries people wear traditional dress. These are the clothes that people in that country have worn for hundreds of years. People also wear special clothes for important occasions such as weddings and funerals.

▲ These Muslim women in Iran are wearing full-length robes because it is a rule of the Islamic religion that women should keep their bodies covered from head to foot.

◀ This Japanese girl is wearing traditional dress, a silk kimono.

SUNBATHING

Less than a hundred years ago people wore bathing costumes that covered most of their bodies. It was not thought to be decent to show too much of your body in public. These costumes were uncomfortable to swim in because they became heavy in water. Now, most holidaymakers wear light, casual clothes or modern swimwear on the beach. Modern swimming costumes are lightweight and fit close to the skin. This makes it easier to swim and play in the sea.

▼ Holidaymakers who spend the day relaxing on the beach or playing in the sea often wear swimming costumes which leave a lot of their bodies uncovered.

Lying in the sun too long can cause sunburn. The skin becomes red and sore. The sun can damage the skin and cause skin cancer. Putting on protective sun cream helps to stop the skin from burning. Your eyes can also be damaged by bright sunlight reflected from the sea and sand. Wearing sun-glasses helps to protect the eyes.

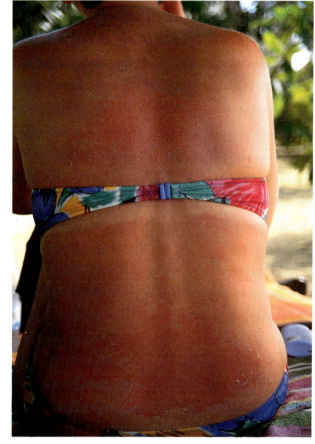

▼ Some people in hot countries, such as those in Africa, decorate their bodies for special occasions with dyes and paints instead of wearing clothes.

▶ This woman's back is badly sunburnt because her skin was left uncovered in the sun for too long.

CLOTHES TO MATCH

CLOTHES TO MATCH LIFE STYLES

People who live in the same climate do not all wear the same type of clothes. It depends upon the way they live, their religion, the jobs they do and how much money they have.

CLIMATES

People who live in hot and cold places need to wear clothes which suit the climate. Look at this map of the world. Find places on or near the Equator. These are the hottest places on Earth along with the deserts of Africa and Australia. Regions with hot climates either have very long, hot summers and short, mild winters or are hot all year round.

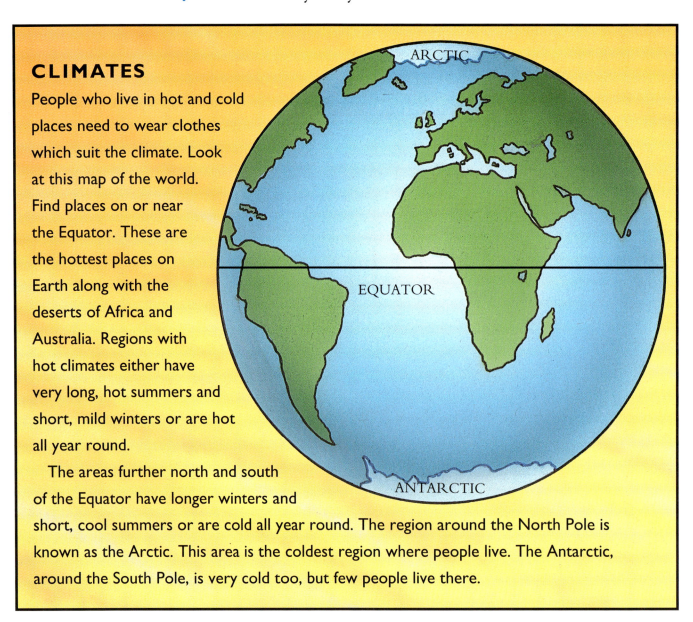

The areas further north and south of the Equator have longer winters and short, cool summers or are cold all year round. The region around the North Pole is known as the Arctic. This area is the coldest region where people live. The Antarctic, around the South Pole, is very cold too, but few people live there.

THE CLIMATE

◀ **This Laplander reindeer herder is wearing an outfit made from reindeer hide. Clothes made from animal skins are hard-wearing and give protection from the cold. The herder's outfit will keep him warm.**

▼ **This family lives in a village which is high in the Himalayan Mountains. There are no shops near by, so people have to make many of their own clothes. The women are knitting scarves and jumpers from wool.**

Somebody who works outdoors in cold weather, such as an Inuit hunter or Laplander reindeer herder, would wear layers of clothes to keep warm and dry. People who work inside, in heated offices and factories, are not affected by the weather outside and can wear light clothes.

People who live in areas that are a long way from towns or cities may have to wear the same clothes for a long time, because it is difficult for them to get to the shops to buy new clothes. They may make their clothes themselves and mend them if they get torn.

NATURAL FIBRES

▲ These people are stretching out a length of washed cotton material to dry in the sun.

A variety of plants which can be made into materials or clothes grow in hot places. Some people from Indonesia and Malaysia even make clothes from the bark of trees. Clothing materials made from plants are called natural fibres. In India people make clothes from natural fibres such as cotton and silk. Silk is a natural fibre but it does not come from a plant. Silk fibres are spun by silkworms.

The basic way of making clothes from natural fibres has not changed for hundreds of years. The natural materials have to be processed (changed) before they can be used. This involves machines which change the original material into fibres and then change the fibres into cloth.

◀ These people are picking cotton in Greece.

▼ This man and girl, in India, are weaving silk threads on a loom to make the cloth for a sari.

HOW COTTON CLOTH IS MADE

Cotton is the most common fibre for making clothes. The cotton crop is picked from the cotton bush. The cotton is stretched and twisted into long, thin threads and gathered on to a spindle. The threads are arranged on a machine called a loom. The loom holds lots of threads, called warp threads, in a vertical line. A horizontal thread of cotton (called a weft thread) is then woven over and under each of the warp threads. This is called weaving. By doing this over and over again cloth is made. Cotton and silk clothes can be made colourful by dyeing the material.

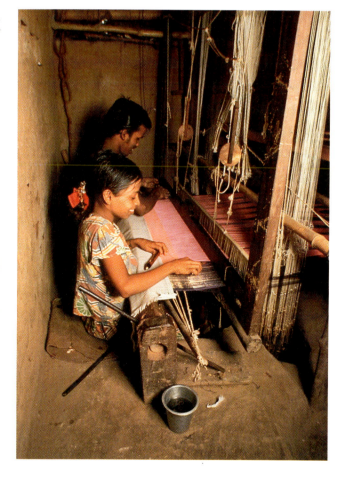

HIDES AND FURS

It is thought that the first clothes humans wore were made from animal hides and furs. Today, animal hides and furs are still used a lot in cold countries to make clothes because they stop the body's heat from escaping. Also, few plants grow in very cold regions of the world, such as the Arctic, so the people who live there have to make clothes from the materials that are available – the hides and furs of animals.

Modern-day Inuits usually live in towns with shops near by, but in the past they would have hunted animals in the frozen countryside. This meant they spent a lot of time in very cold conditions. Traditional Inuit clothes are made from many kinds of animal hides and furs. The most important is the hide of the caribou (the North American name for reindeer), from which they make large overcoats with hoods which cover the head. The hoods are lined with polar bear fur. Caribou hide is very light, which makes it comfortable to move and

► **This Inuit woman from Alaska is wearing a traditional fur outfit.**

work in. Underneath the overcoat the Inuit sometimes wear a vest made from birds' skins sewn together. The vest and overcoat trap the body's heat. To keep their feet warm and dry, the Inuit wear waterproof boots made from sealskin, which are lined with polar bear fur.

People who live in hot places also use animal hides and furs. Native Americans from the plains of the USA traditionally made clothes out of the hides of buffalo (a type of large cattle). The skins were rubbed with oil and left to dry in the sun. The buffalo hides were then stretched and sewn together to make clothing. Sometimes feathers and fur were used as decoration and also to make head-dresses.

▲ These native Americans are performing a traditional dance wearing outfits made from buffalo hides and animal furs.

SYNTHETIC MATERIAL

► **This US soldier works in the cold climate of the Arctic, so he is wearing warm, waterproof clothing made from synthetic material.**

▼ **Synthetic material can be made into many types of clothing. This girl is wearing a plastic overcoat and a pair of boots to keep dry in the rain.**

Instead of using natural materials, such as plants and animal hides, scientists have been able to produce synthetic materials to make clothes. Most synthetic materials, such as nylon and plastic, are made from chemicals which come from oil.

In cold and wet places synthetic materials are used to make warm, waterproof clothing. The uniforms worn by soldiers based in Alaska, USA, have copied the style of the traditional hunting clothes of the Inuit, but the soldiers' clothes are synthetic.

The waterproof trousers and jackets are made from special nylon and are lined with nylon fur material.

Plastics have been used to make waterproof clothing for many years. Plastic can be stretched into sheets which can then be cut to size and made into almost any kind of clothing, such as hats, overcoats and boots.

WHAT ARE YOUR CLOTHES MADE FROM?

Synthetic materials can be dyed different colours or made to look like natural materials, such as leather, fur and wool. Sometimes synthetic materials are mixed with natural fibres to make clothes. If you look at the labels in shop-bought clothes you will see what materials have been used. You could make a list of the materials in the clothes you wear and see if most of your clothes are made from all natural fibres, synthetic materials or a mixture of both. Put the information in a box like this.

ITEM OF CLOTHING	MATERIAL	SYNTHETIC	NATURAL FIBRES	BOTH
JUMPER	ACRYLIC	✔		
CARDIGAN	WOOL		✔	
SOCKS	ACRYLIC/ COTTON			✔
VEST	COTTON		✔	
TIE	NYLON	✔		
SHOES	LEATHER		✔	

HOW CLOTHES KEEP US WARM

▼ This man's thick fur cloak and hat will keep him warm because it will stop his body heat from escaping.

If it is very cold you need to keep warm. The best way of keeping warm is to keep in the heat that your body makes. If a fabric keeps in the heat it is called an insulator. But the best insulator is air! When you are cold, you probably wear lots of layers of clothes. Most people think that the fabric is keeping them warm. But it is really all the layers of warm air trapped between the clothes!

KEEPING WARM

Have you ever worn a string vest or thermal underwear? These are designed to keep sweat, which cools the skin, away from the body. The tiny holes in the material trap the warm air so your skin is kept dry and warm.

Fur coats or clothing and boots lined with fur, such as those worn by Inuits in the Arctic, work in the same way. The fur traps the warm air so that the heat from the person's body does not escape.

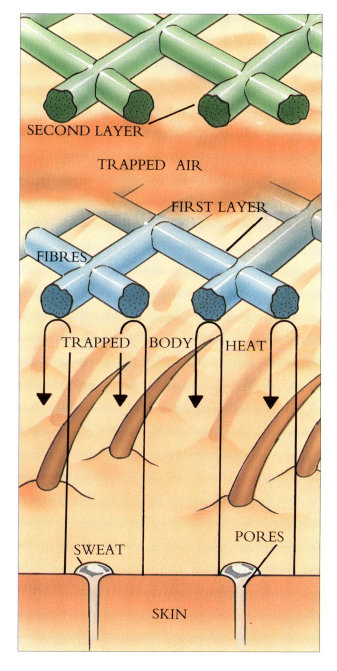

SECOND LAYER

TRAPPED AIR

FIRST LAYER

FIBRES

TRAPPED BODY HEAT

SWEAT

PORES

SKIN

◄ This artwork shows how difficult it is for heat from the body to escape through the air trapped between the layers of clothing.

▲ This woman is wearing the typical dress of the people who live in the mountain regions of Peru. In high mountain areas the wind is very cold even when it is sunny – so people wear many layers of clothes to keep warm.

HOW CLOTHES KEEP US COOL

▲ These men from North Africa are wearing loose-fitting clothes. White material reflects the sun's heat from their bodies.

People in hot places usually wear loose clothes to keep cool. If they wore tight clothes all the warm air would stay close to their skin and they would get too hot. Loose clothes float about and let cool air near the skin. The cool air takes away the heat from the person's body, which helps the body to stay at the right temperature.

In hot, desert regions of the Middle East and North Africa people often wear white clothes. White reflects the sun's heat from the body, so the person does not get too hot.

Indian women wear saris which are made from single lengths of cotton or silk cloth wrapped around their bodies. They also have a section of cloth that can be thrown over the head and shoulders. Saris can be loosened or tightened depending upon how hot or cold the weather is. Indian men wear a similar wraparound garment called a dhoti. This is a length of material which is wrapped around the waist and between the legs.

COOLING DOWN

Sweating is a very important way of cooling down. Sweat is mostly water. When you sweat the water takes the heat from the skin and makes the air moist. This helps the body to cool down.

In hot, dry places people wear loose clothes, which allow the air to move around their bodies to make a cooling breeze. The sweaty, warm air is replaced by fresh air. The body can then carry on sweating.

In really hot, wet places, such as the Amazon rain forest, people leave their skin uncovered. Cool breezes take the sweat away from their bodies. This helps to keep them at the right temperature.

▶ **These women in Nepal are wearing beautifully coloured saris. When it is hot the material can be loosened to let in cool air.**

HEAD-DRESSES

▶ This Indian man is wearing a colourful turban.

Head-dresses are worn over the head – they can be lengths of fabric wrapped around the head or hats. They may be worn for protection against the heat or cold or just for decoration. Some people have to keep their heads covered by a hat or head-dress for religious reasons.

Arab men in North Africa wear turbans, which are lengths of cloth wrapped round and round the head. This keeps the sun off the head. Some Muslim men in

North African countries, such as Morocco or Egypt, wear a hat without a brim, called a fez. When Muslim men pray they kneel down and put their heads to the ground – if their hats had brims they would get in the way.

In China and south-east Asia, farmworkers spend a lot of time working in the sun, so they wear hats with wide brims which cast shadows over the wearer. It is like being in the shade all day. A similar hat, called a sombrero, is worn in Mexico.

▲ This man's sheepskin hat will help to keep him warm.

◄ These tea-pickers from Indonesia are wearing wide-brimmed straw hats to shade them from the sun.

FOOTWEAR

▲ **This reindeer herder from Lapland is repairing his shoe made from reindeer hide.**

One place where we lose a lot of heat from our bodies is our feet. When our feet are too cold we feel cold all over. This is why it is important for people living in cold regions to keep their feet warm. In cold places, such as Lapland, northern Russia and the Arctic, people wear thick boots to stop getting wet and cold in the deep snow. These boots usually come right up to the knee. They are often made from leather because it is strong and hard-wearing. Laplanders and Inuits use reindeer hides or sealskins. In Tibet, boots are made from the hides of yaks (long-haired cattle).

Although Tibetans wear thick woollen socks, the boots may also be lined with fur for extra warmth.

Some people who have to travel over deep snow use special snow-shoes. These do not look like shoes at all; they are made from a wooden frame, crisscrossed with leather thongs. They look like big tennis rackets strapped to the feet. The design of snow-shoes means that the body's weight is spread over a bigger area than the feet alone – so the person does not sink into the snow so much and it is easier to walk.

In hot places it is important to keep the feet cool. Amazon Indians do not wear shoes at all. In desert areas the ground gets too hot to walk on without shoes, so people living there wear sandals. Their sandals have flat soles, usually made from wood, which are held on to the foot by straps. They are loose-fitting and leave a lot of the foot exposed to the air which makes them cool to wear. Some native Americans make shoes, called moccasins, from buffalo skin. The leather is shaped to wrap around the foot and ankle in one piece. Moccasins are easy to make but they wear out quickly.

▼ **This Inuit is wearing snow-shoes. They make walking in deep snow much easier for him.**

SPORTSWEAR

Many people like to exercise and play sports. Outdoor sports often involve a lot of moving about. When we exercise, our bodies become hot and we sweat to cool down. Sportspeople wear loose vests and shorts so that air can move around the body and dry the sweat.

In Kenya and Ethiopia, in Africa, long-distance running is a popular sport. People run between villages which are often many kilometres apart. Running these distances in such a hot climate could be very uncomfortable, but loose clothing which allows the air to move about the body keeps the runners cool.

▼ Athletes wear light vests and shorts when they compete.

◀ **Skiers need to wear tight-fitting clothes to make sure the wind does not slow them down.**

Water sports, such as surfing and water-skiing, are popular in hot countries. Although the sun is very hot, the sea is much colder, so surfers not only have to wear T-shirts to protect their skin from the sun, but also wet suits to keep them warm in the cold sea.

Some sports take place in cold places, for example snow skiing in the Alps during winter. Skiers have to wear clothes that will keep them warm and that are padded to protect the elbows and knees in case they fall on the hard, packed snow.

In competitions, skiers try to go down snow- and ice-covered mountains as quickly as they can. If they wore loose clothing it would catch the wind and slow them down, so they wear clothes which fit closely to their bodies and allow them to move faster.

WORKING CLOTHES

So far we have looked at some clothes in hot and cold climates. There are other places where people work which may be very hot or very cold. People have to wear clothes that suit their work and workplace. For example, firefighters have to wear special clothes that help to protect them against the heat of a fire. Sometimes they use special equipment which helps them to breathe if an area is filled with smoke or if there are poisonous fumes produced from a fire.

Steel mills are very hot places to work in because the furnaces which melt down the metal need to be at

▲ **Firefighters sometimes have to wear special fire-resistant suits which cover all of the body and face.**

▶ **Steel mill workers pouring hot, molten metal.**

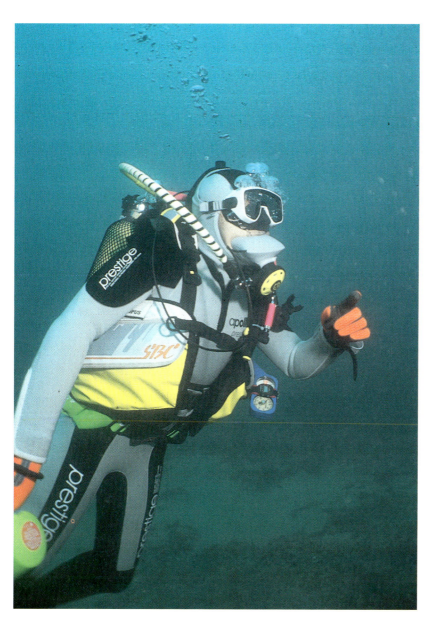

▼ **This scuba diver is wearing a wet suit to keep warm in the sea.**

very high temperatures. Also, a lot of heat comes from the molten (melted) metal as it is sent along different machines to be made into sheets of steel. It is very hot and uncomfortable to work in these conditions, but the steel mill workers cannot leave too much skin bare to cool down because of the danger from sparks or splashes of hot metal. People who work with hot materials have to wear protective clothing, such as fire-resistant overalls, gloves, hard hats and tinted goggles to protect the eyes.

Some people work in very cold places. Scuba divers often work deep underwater in very cold seas. To protect their bodies from the cold they wear wet suits made of synthetic rubber, which trap a small layer of water close to the body. The body warms the water and the warmed water acts like a blanket, keeping the divers warm. It is hard to see under the water, so divers wear goggles which keep the water out of their eyes.

WASHING AND DRYING

▼ **This oil rig worker's dirty and oil-stained clothes will need to be cleaned with strong detergents (soaps) and hot water.**

Most clothes need to be washed at some time or another. How often clothes are washed depends upon how often they are worn and how easy they are to dry. Our clothes pick up dirt, stains and the sweat from our bodies. Germs build up in dirty clothes so washing them is a way of staying healthy. Clothes, such as underwear, which come in contact with our bodies the most, need to be washed more often.

In many hot countries people wash their clothes in rivers or streams. Clothes have been washed this way since people started wearing clothing. The garments are scrubbed and beaten against rocks to get them clean and are left to dry in the hot sun. Washing in warm or hot water kills the germs and cleans off stains quicker than cold water. This is why people washing clothes in rivers and streams have to scrub their clothes to get them clean. The clothes dry quickly in the warm air so they can be worn again almost straight away.

In cold places people wear many layers. Only the underwear needs to be washed regularly. In Canada, and other developed countries which have cold climates, most people have washing machines. The machines use warm or hot water and detergents to get the clothes clean without the need to scrub the

◀ These men are washing their clothes in a river in Malaysia.

▼ These lengths of cloth are drying on a washing line in Sri Lanka.

material. Although clothes can sometimes be dried outside in cold climates, usually they are dried indoors in special hot cupboards or in tumble driers. These are machines that blow hot air on to clothes as they turn in a drum.

GLOSSARY

brim The edge of a hat.

cancer A disease that affects body cells so that they grow too quickly.

decent Proper and acceptable way of acting or dressing.

deserts Areas that have very little plant life growing in them. They are usually found in regions with a hot and dry climate.

Equator The imaginary line that circles the centre of the Earth. The hottest areas of the Earth are around the Equator.

exposed Left unprotected.

fibres Fine threads of material.

fire-resistant A material which does not burn easily.

furnaces Enclosed structures, like very big ovens, in which great heat is produced.

germs Very tiny forms of animal or plant life that can cause disease.

hide The skin of an animal.

insulator A material that does not allow heat to pass through.

loom A machine for weaving thread into cloth. Threads are stretched from the top to the bottom of the loom and then a thread is passed from side to side and is threaded under and over each of these threads.

reflecting When light bounces off a surface or material.

scuba The breathing equipment used by divers. Scuba divers wear containers filled with air on their backs. As they swim underwater they can breathe this air through the tube and mouthpiece which lead from the containers.

spindle A thin rod on which thread is twisted and wound so that it can be used on a loom to be woven into cloth.

synthetic Something that has not been grown or formed naturally.

wet suits Suits, worn by divers, made from special rubber that allows a thin layer of water to collect between the body and the suit. The water is warmed by the body's heat and this keeps the diver warm as he or she swims in the sea.

FURTHER READING

Costumes and Clothes by Jean Cooke (Wayland, 1986)
Costumes and Clothes series by Miriam Moss (Wayland, 1988)
Just Look at Clothes by Brenda Ralph Lewis (Macdonald Educational, 1985)

PICTURE ACKNOWLEDGEMENTS

Bryan and Cherry Alexander *cover* (top), 4, 9 (top), 13 (D. Corner), 14 (top), 22, 23; Allsport *title page*, 25 (B. Martin); Collections 6 (P. Watts); Robert Estall Photographs 7 (bottom) (A. Fisher/ C. Beckwith), 18 (A. Fisher); Eye Ubiquitous *cover* (bottom) (D. Cumming), 5 (bottom) (F. Leather), 7 (top) (P. Seheult), 9 (bottom) (D. Cumming), 10 (D. Cumming), 11 (top) (J. Waterlow), 21 (bottom) (S. Coe), 27 (A.G. Tornero), 29 (top) (J. Hulme), 29 (bottom) (P. Field); Link Picture Library 19 (S. Kessler); Magnum Pictures 5 (top) (Abbas), 12 (D. Stock); Tony Stone Worldwide 24 (B.Robbins), 26 (bottom right) 28; Topham Picture Library 11 (bottom), 17; ZEFA 14 (bottom), 16 (Steenmans), 20, 21 (top), 26 (top left). All artwork by David Price.

INDEX

Numbers in **bold** indicate
entries which are illustrated.